GRATITUDE IS THE ANSWER

The Secret To Happiness

ALSO BY JAQUI KARR:

"SOLACE FROM DEPRESSION"
A BOOK THAT IS A PLACE OF SOLACE, SUPPORT, UNDERSTANDING, AND COMPASSION - BALANCED WITH NUTRITIONAL INFORMATION THAT IS RELEVANT AND IMMEDIATELY APPLICABLE.

BESIDES THE DIFFICULTIES OF LIFE IN GENERAL, OUR ENVIRONMENT CAN MAKE US TRULY ILL OR WEAKEN OUR SYSTEM TO A POINT THAT MAKES IT A CHALLENGE TO COPE. LEARN HOW YOUR HEALTH CAN BE IMMEDIATELY IMPROVED.

YOU CAN'T BEAT SOMETHING THAT YOU DON'T UNDERSTAND. LEARN HOW TO NOURISH YOUR BODY PROPERLY AND NATURALLY SO THAT YOU CAN GIVE YOURSELF THE STRENGTH AND PHYSIOLOGICAL ADVANTAGE TO WIN.

DECIDE *TODAY* THAT YOU WANT TO LIVE A HAPPIER LIFE.

AVAILABLE FROM AMAZON.COM
AND OTHER RETAILERS

Gratitude isn't always easy. We all *know* we should be thankful for what we have regardless of how much or how little, we know there are others all over the world who are living in unfathomable conditions, yet others who are our neighbors battling terrible challenges and illnesses...yet somehow, it still isn't always easy to stay in a state of constant gratitude.

Feeling gratitude is such an important key to being in a state of happiness. Not just feeling happy moments every now and then, but actually living in a constant content happy state. Gratitude helps us to exist in a form of consciousness that allows for more. It allows for things to flow and work freely around us, not constricted or blocked by negative thoughts and negative feelings.

This book is meant to do many things:

...offer inspiration for those difficult days...

...be a reminder of tiny miracles that we sometimes forget...

...provide a positive place to immediately travel to...

...be the keeper of your beautiful thoughts and

emotions when they appear...

-but most importantly, be an instrument to help keep you in a state of gratitude as much as possible and help you to rediscover the beauty that is already in your life and connect to higher, more positive energies.

These pages are all yours: write, scribble, doodle, jot, draw everywhere! I have shared my journal with you in the hope that perhaps a thought or a single word will help connect you to something you have become disconnected from, perhaps discover joy and pleasure from something you never noticed before.

When we surround ourselves with love and appreciation,

more appears

May more always appear for you

Jaqui Karr

JaquiKarr.com

I AM SO GRATEFUL FOR THIS MOMENT

T-H-I-S VERY MOMENT

THIS VERY BREATH

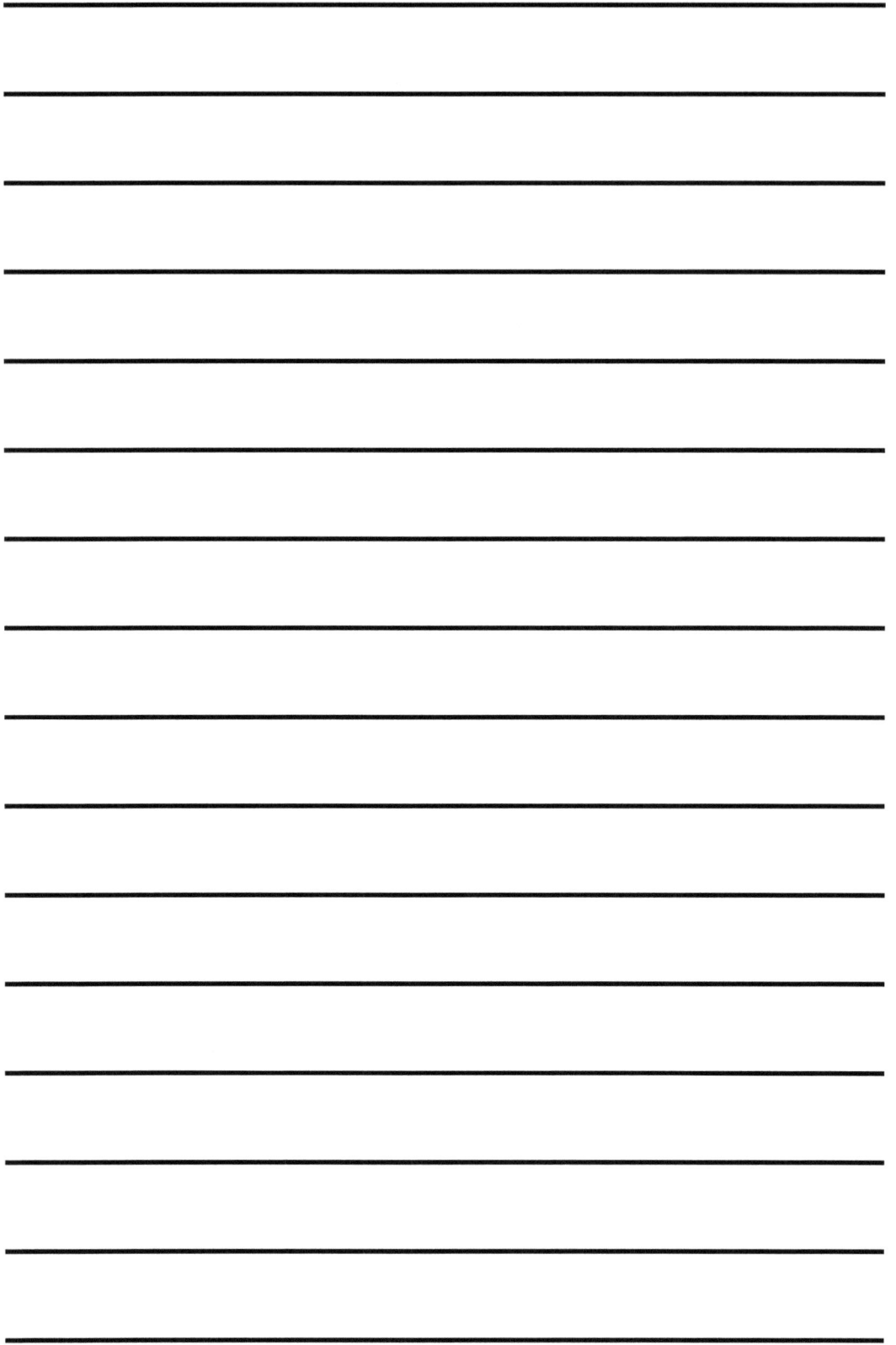

THANK YOU FOR THE

GREAT LOVE

THAT FILLS MY HEART

SOMETIMES WITH THE GREATEST PAIN

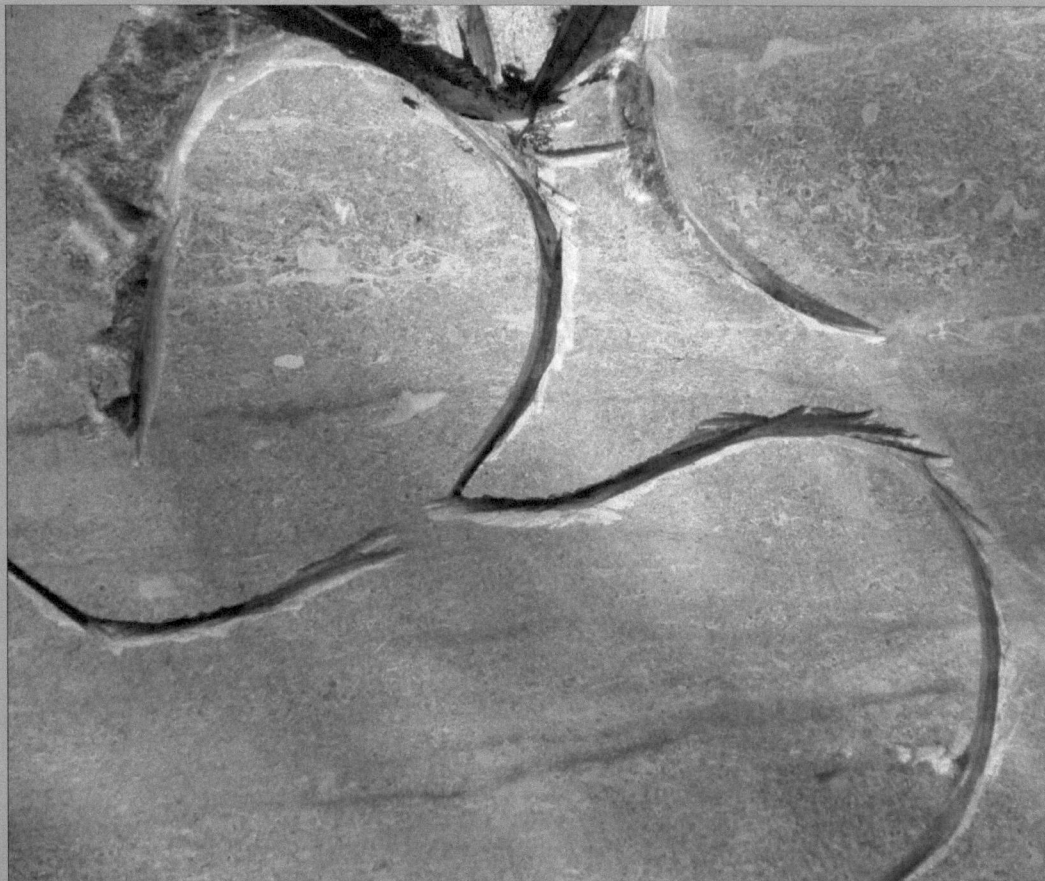

THANK YOU FOR

THE PAIN

THAT TEACHES ME

WHAT GREAT LOVE IS

I AM INFINITELY GRATEFUL FOR

FREEDOM

AND THE ABILITY

TO CHOOSE

I LOVE HOW THE SUN AND MOON MAKE THEIR WAY
INTO A ROOM. THEIR RAYS OF LIGHT REMIND US THAT
THERE IS ALWAYS LIGHT AND HOPE
REGARDLESS OF ALL THE TRANSIENT DARKNESS.

THANK YOU FOR WATER

WATER
RIVERS
OCEANS
RAIN
THAT CAN WASH AWAY ANYTHING

TIDES THAT PROMISE US
A NEW BEGINNING TO
EACH AND EVERY DAY

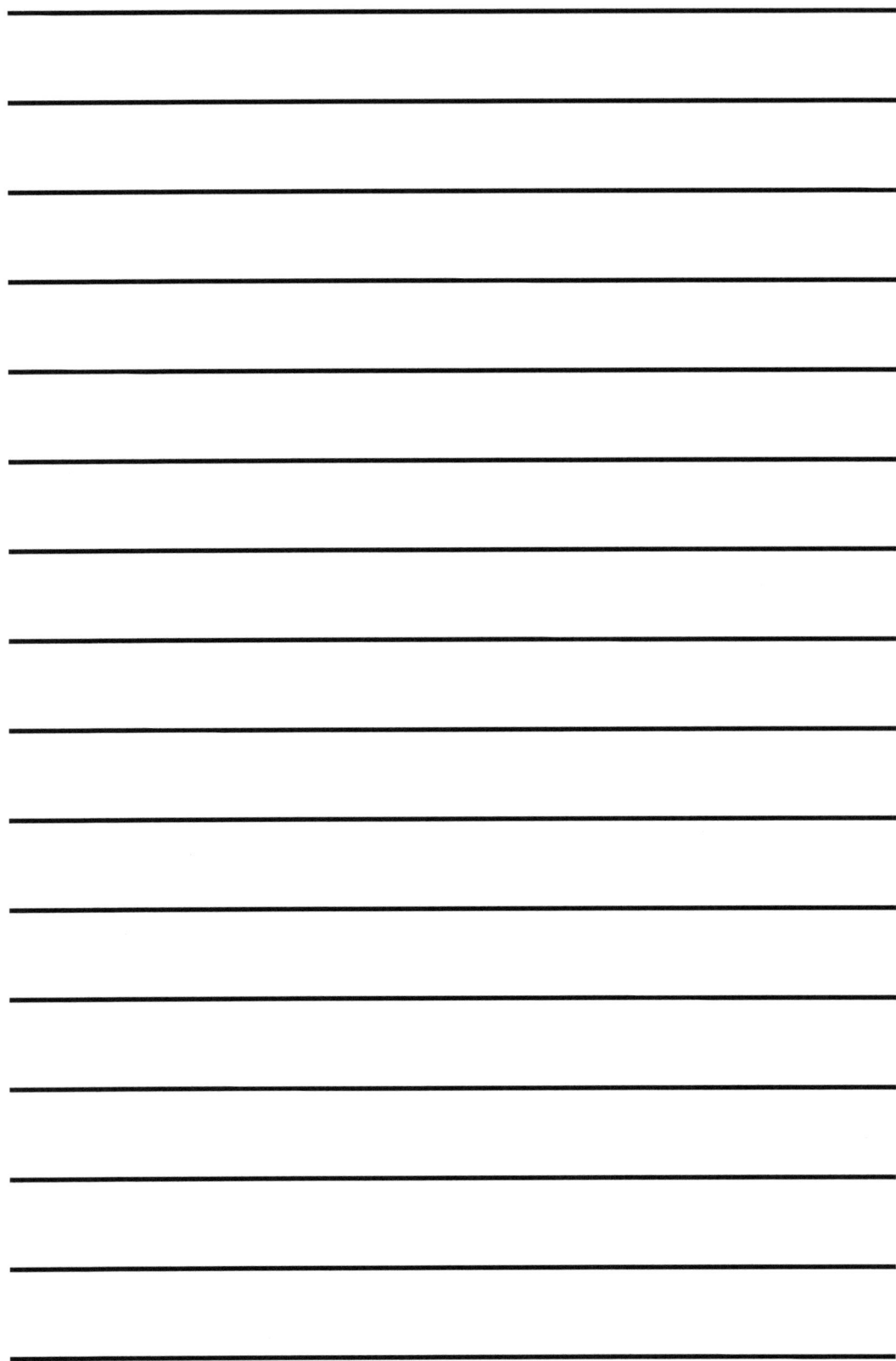

I AM SO GRATEFUL FOR THE PERFECTION OF
SEEMING IMPERFECTIONS

THAT REMIND US TO
JUST BE

AND ALLOW OTHERS
TO ALSO JUST BE

EVERY LAST THING ON EARTH IS VITAL
TO SOMETHING OR SOMEONE ELSE

EVERYTHING AND EVERYONE ARE
COMPLETELY PERFECT JUST AS THEY ARE

AT TIMES WE CAN BLIND OURSELVES BY LOOKING TOO HARD FOR BEAUTY AND HAPPINESS. THINGS THAT WE PERCEIVE TO BE IN THE WAY OF OUR SUNSHINE ARE JUST AS BEAUTIFUL AS WHAT WE ARE SEARCHING FOR.

THANK YOU FOR CONTINUALLY BRINGING BEAUTY TO OUR DAYS AND ALLOWING US WHATEVER TIME WE NEED TO RECOGNIZE AND APPRECIATE IT.

THANK YOU FOR FRIENDSHIPS
THEY GIVE US SO MUCH
COMFORT
CONSOLATION
LOVE
LAUGHTER
EMPATHY
ACCEPTANCE
SAFETY

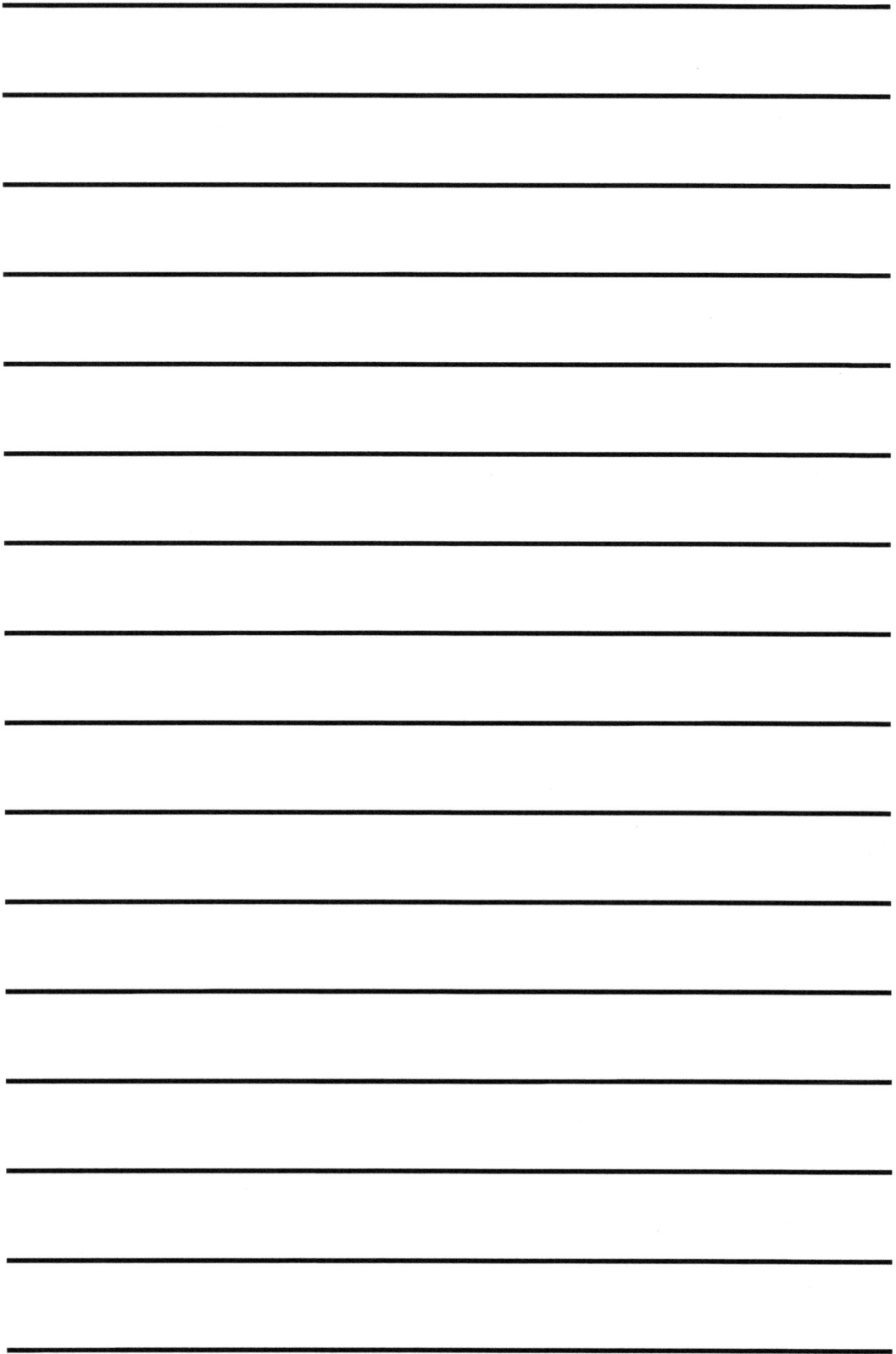

THANK YOU FOR ALL THE TALENTS
IN ME AND IN EACH AND EVERY
PERSON ON EARTH

MAY EACH AND EVERY ONE OF US
DISCOVER OUR GIFTS AND
REALIZE THEM TO FULL
POTENTIAL

THANK YOU FOR MUSIC
IT FEEDS MY SOUL

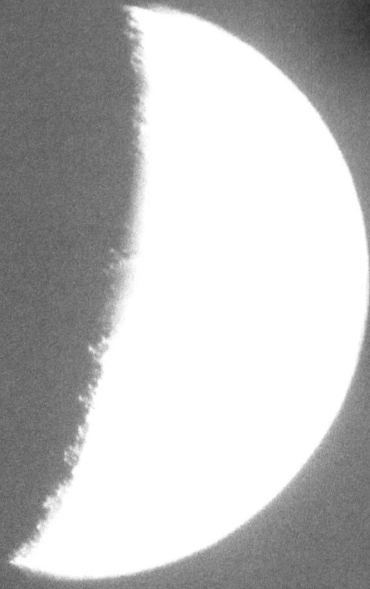

THANK YOU FOR THE INCREDIBLY DEEP RICH COLORS OF
THE SKY JUST BEFORE DAWN; THAT SMALL SPACE OF TIME
BETWEEN DARKNESS AND LIGHT WHEN THE BRILLIANT
STARS SPARKLE AGAINST SAPPHIRE BLUE

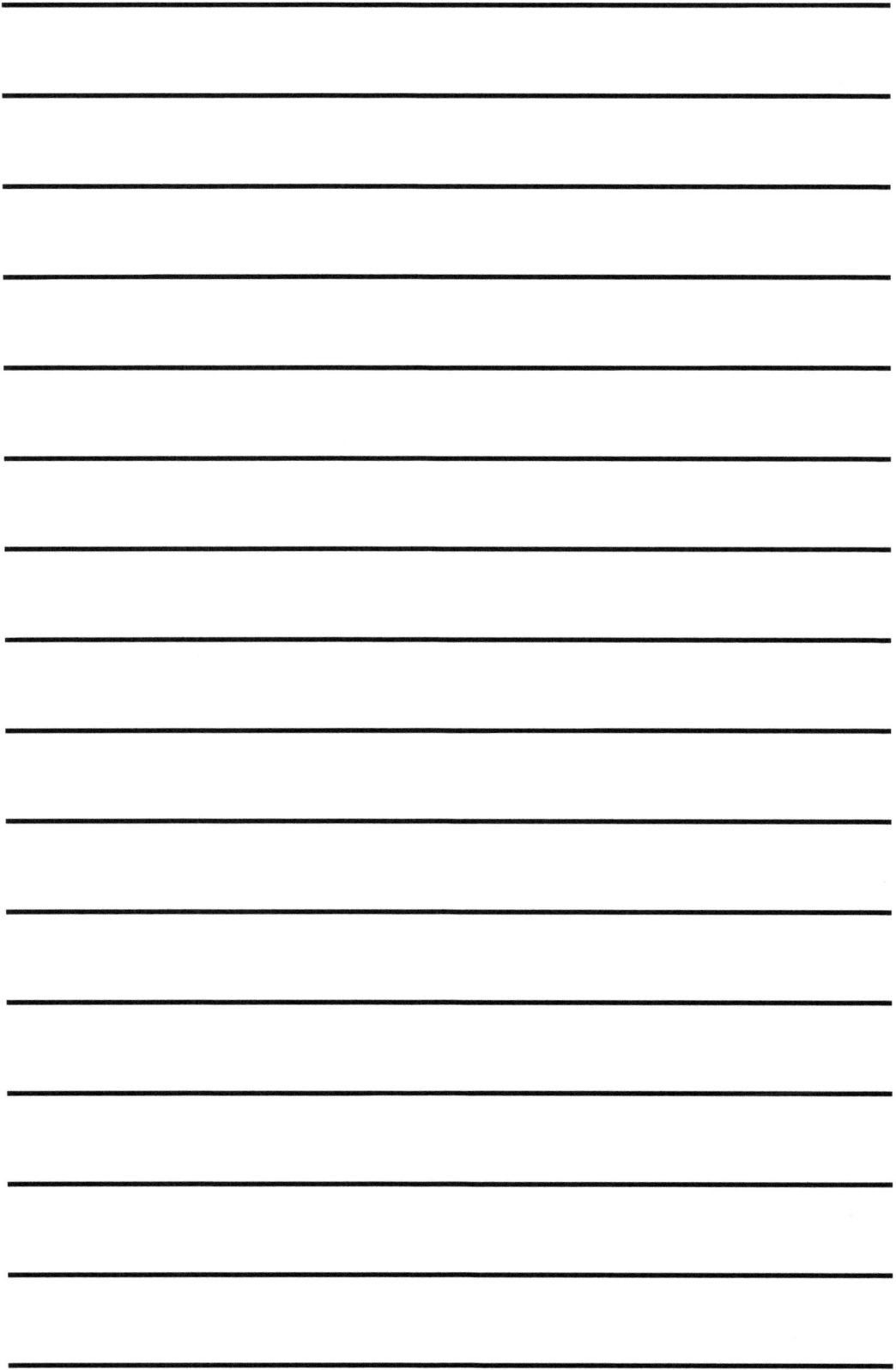

_____

_____

_____

_____

_____

_____

_____

_____

_____

_____

_____

_____

I ABSOLUTELY LOVE THE BEAUTY OF SNOW,
DAZZLING LIKE MILLIONS OF JEWELS,
BEAUTIFYING EVERYTHING, BRINGING SERENITY
TO EVERYTHING FROM ROOFTOPS TO TREES

_____

_____

_____

_____

_____

_____

_____

_____

_____

_____

_____

_____

_____

_____

_____

I LOVE HOW LIGHTING

THE

TINIEST

CANDLE

CAN BRING LIGHT AND LIFE INTO ANY SPACE

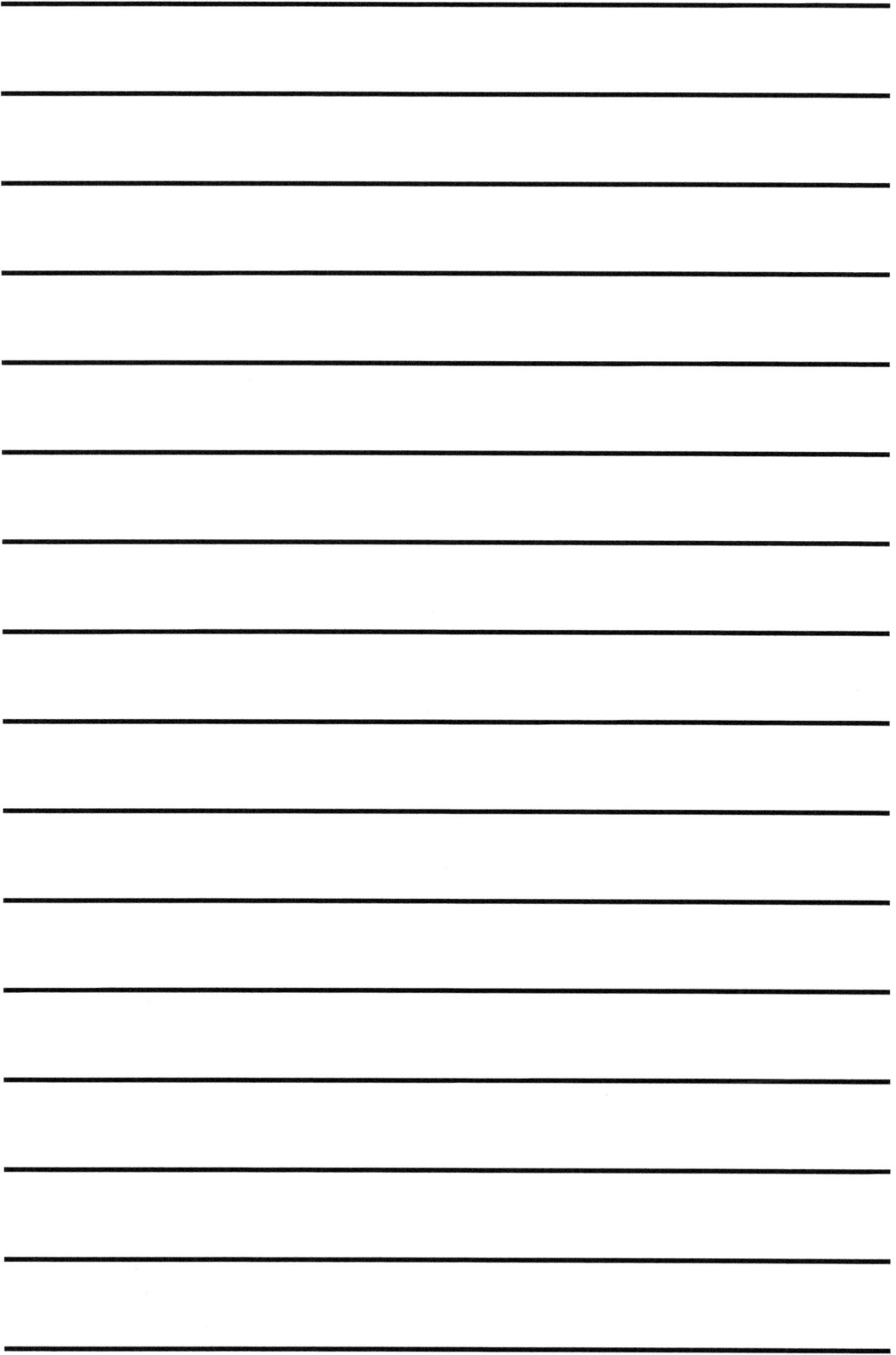

_____

_____

_____

_____

_____

_____

_____

_____

_____

THANK YOU FOR THE INNOCENCE OF CREATURES, THEIR PURITY, THEIR ENERGY THAT OFFERS BALANCE TO OUR SOMETIMES TANGLED STATE

_____

_____

_____

_____

_____

_____

_____

_____

_____

_____

_____

THANK YOU FOR THE FEELING OF HOPE

AT MOMENTS IT CAN BE
ALL
WE
HAVE

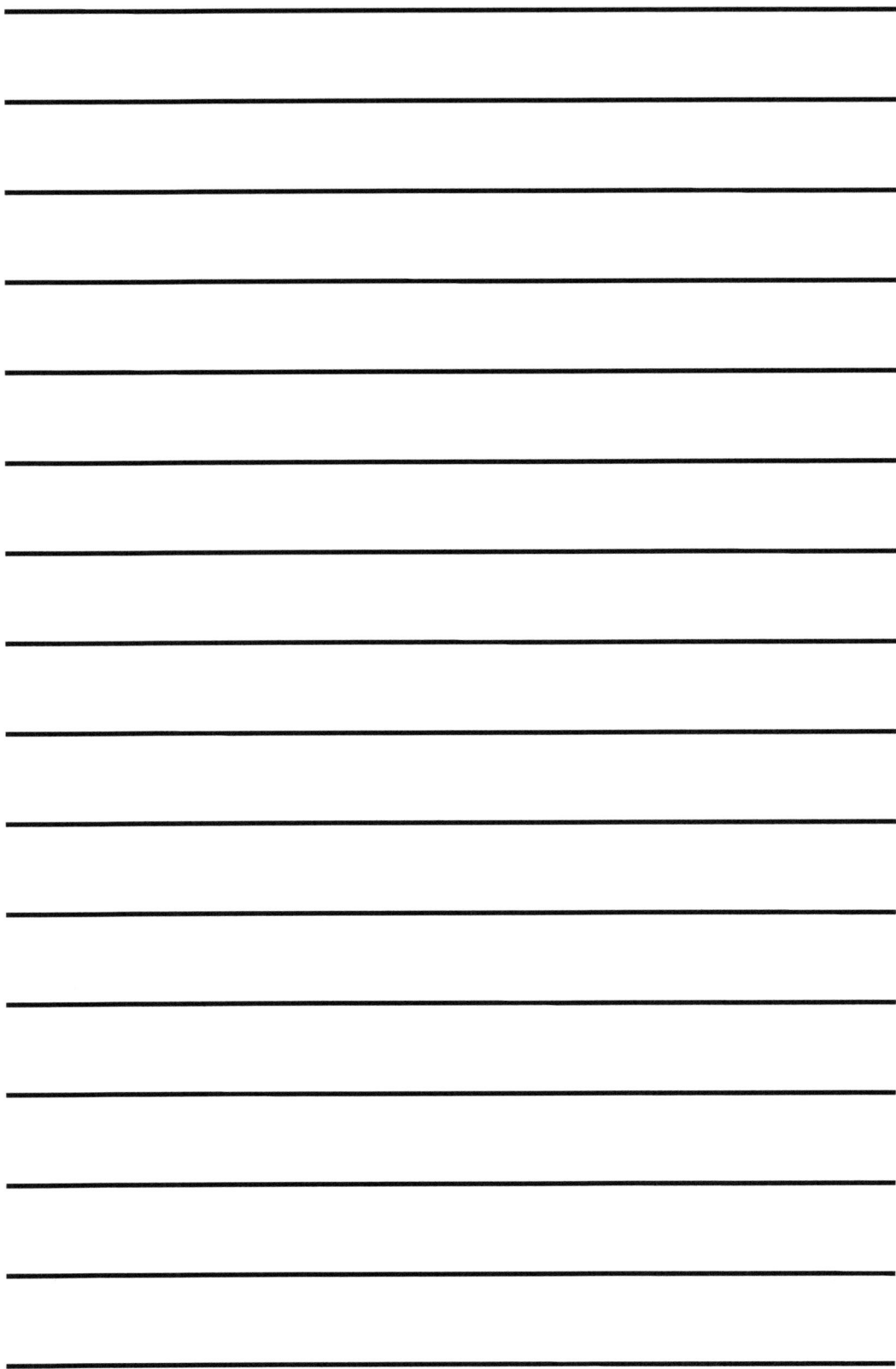

_____

_____

_____

_____

_____

_____

_____

_____

_____

_____

_____

_____

_____

THANK YOU FOR DANCE

IT ALLOWS US TO MOVE AND BECOME THE WIND

WE ARE FREE WHEN WE DANCE

_____

_____

_____

_____

_____

_____

_____

_____

_____

_____

_____

_____

_____

_____

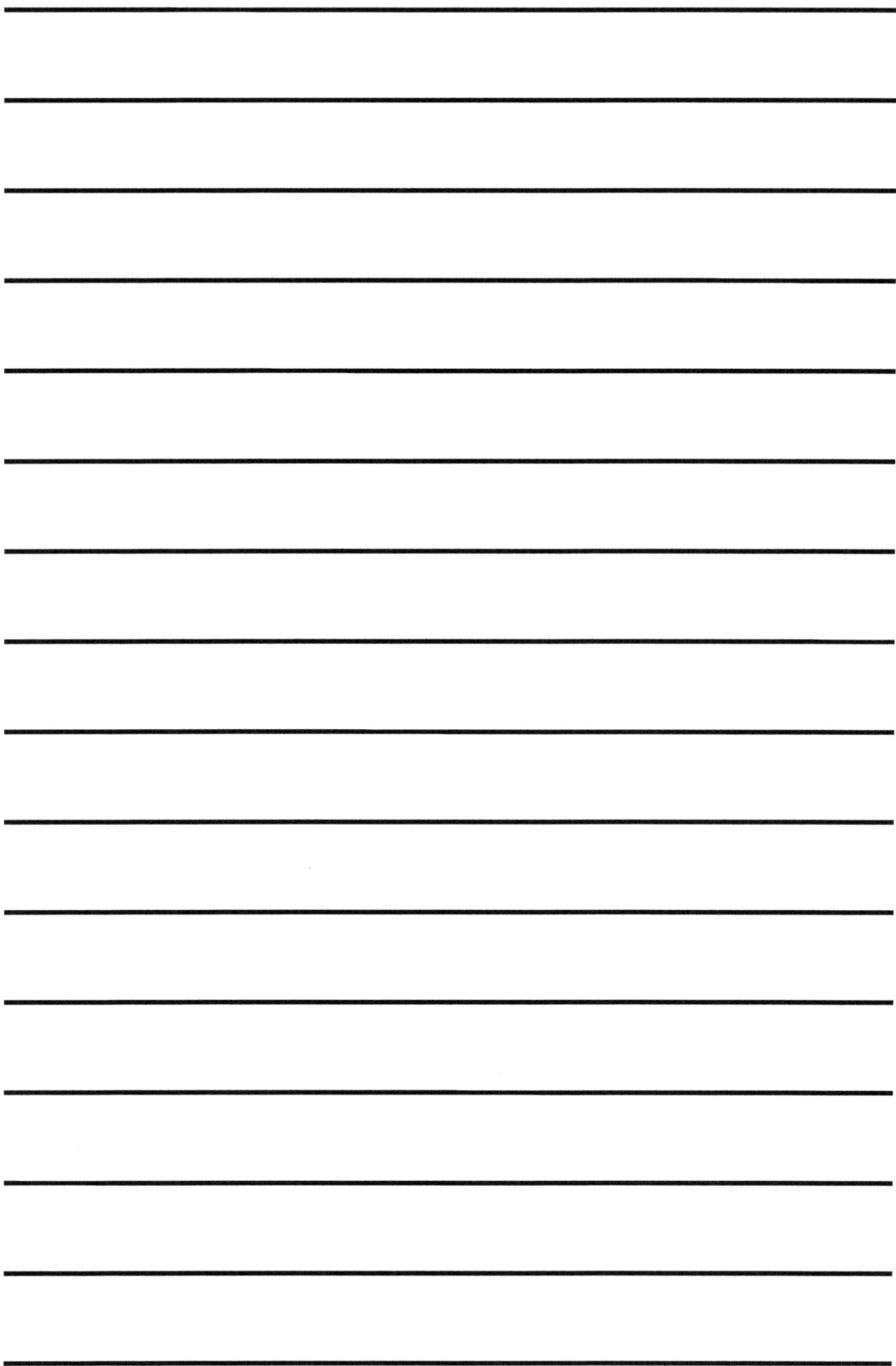

THANK YOU FOR ENDLESS POSSIBILITIES

SOMETIMES WE ARE DRAWN TO PATHS THAT
HAVE NO CLEAR DESTINATION.

PERHAPS WE NEED TO GO THERE ANYWAYS.
PERHAPS SOMETHING WILL MEET US THERE.

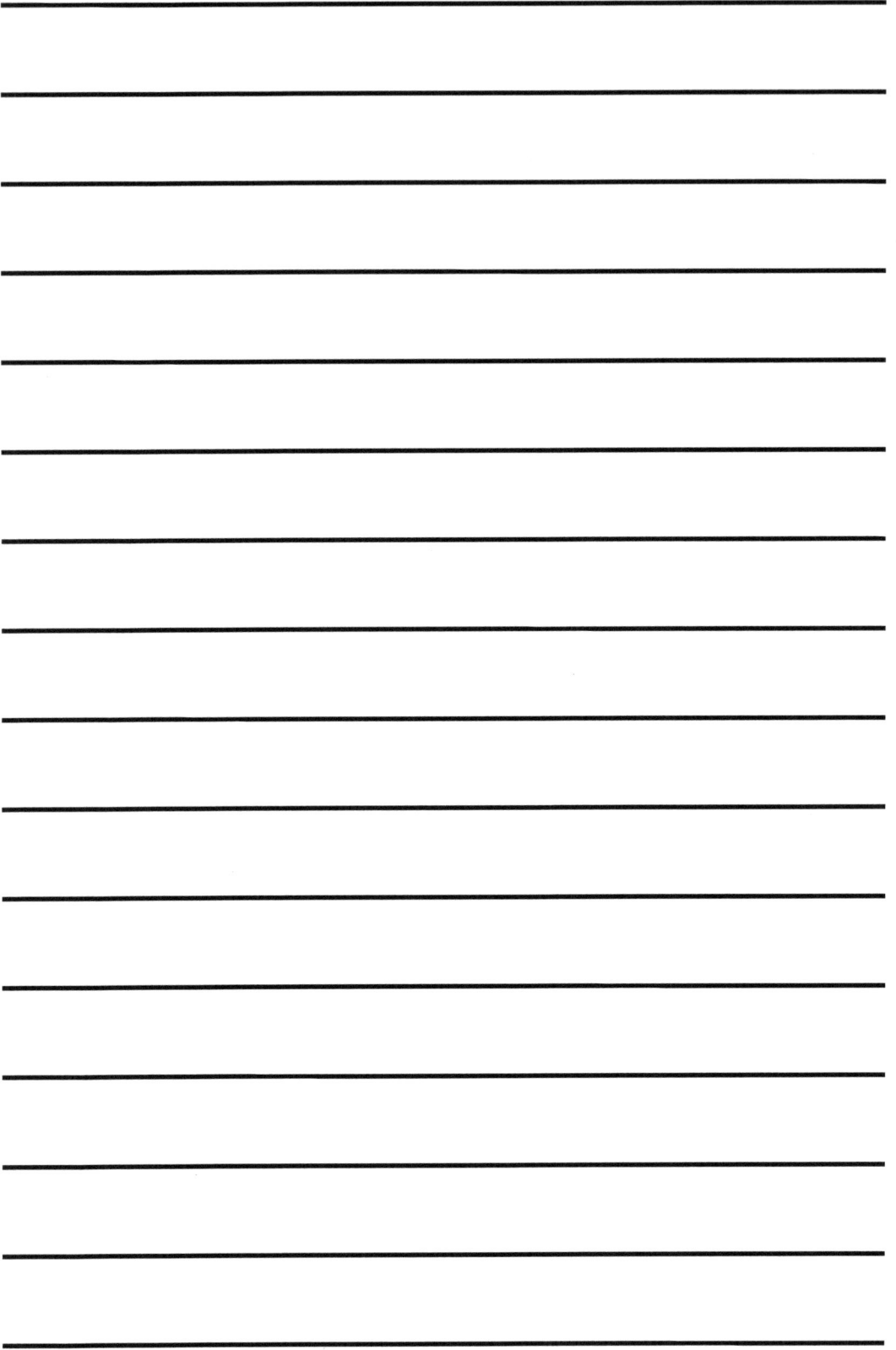

I AM SO VERY GRATEFUL FOR ALL THE LOVING PEOPLE
WHO I HAVE BEEN BLESSED TO HAVE IN MY LIFE

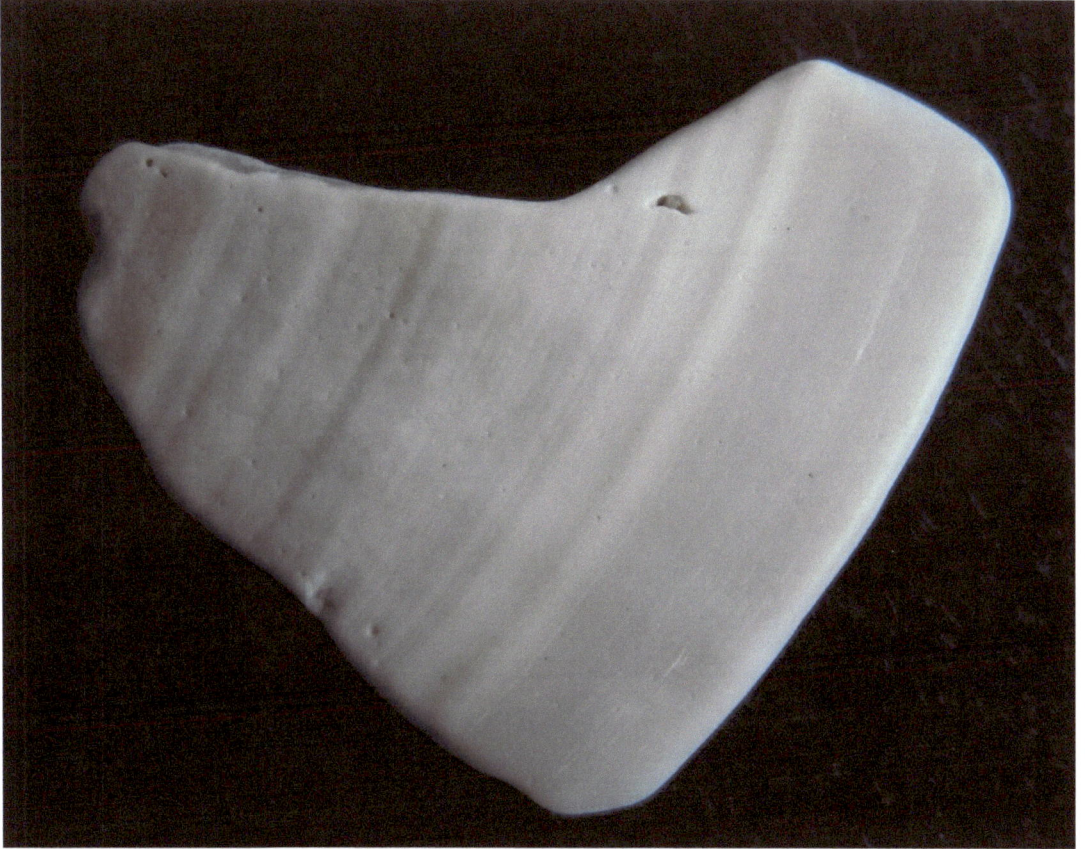

I AM GRATEFUL TO EVERY FRIEND, FAMILY MEMBER,
EVERY
SINGLE
STRANGER
WHO EVER ENRICHED MY DAY WITH THEIR SMILE,
HELD A DOOR, GAVE ME AN INSTANT OF THEMSELVES

THANK YOU FOR ALL THE KINDNESS AND THE LITTLE
ANGELS THAT HAVE CROSSED MY PATH ALONG THE WAY
…SOMETIMES WITHOUT ME EVEN REALIZING IT

THANK YOU FOR FOOD ON THE TABLE TODAY
THANK YOU FOR EVERY BITE, EVERY DROP

MAY WE ALL BE KIND ENOUGH TO SHARE

_____

_____

_____

_____

_____

_____

_____

_____

_____

_____

_____

_____

I LOVE THE SOOTHING EFFECTS OF TEA
THE COMFORT AND HEALING OF HOT COCOA
THE AROMA OF RICH AND DELICIOUS COFFEE

THANK YOU FOR EVERY LEAF, EVERY BEAN

I AM GRATEFUL EVERY DAY FOR THE STRONG BODY
YOU HAVE GIVEN ME TO CARRY MY SOUL.

IT IS RESILIENT AND CAN GET THROUGH ANYTHING

THANK YOU FOR THE ROOF OVER MY HEAD

ALL CREATURES BIG AND SMALL NEED SHELTER

WHETHER IT IS A HOUSE,
OR SHELTER UNDER A LEAF,
WE ALL NEED A TINY SPACE
TO CALL HOME

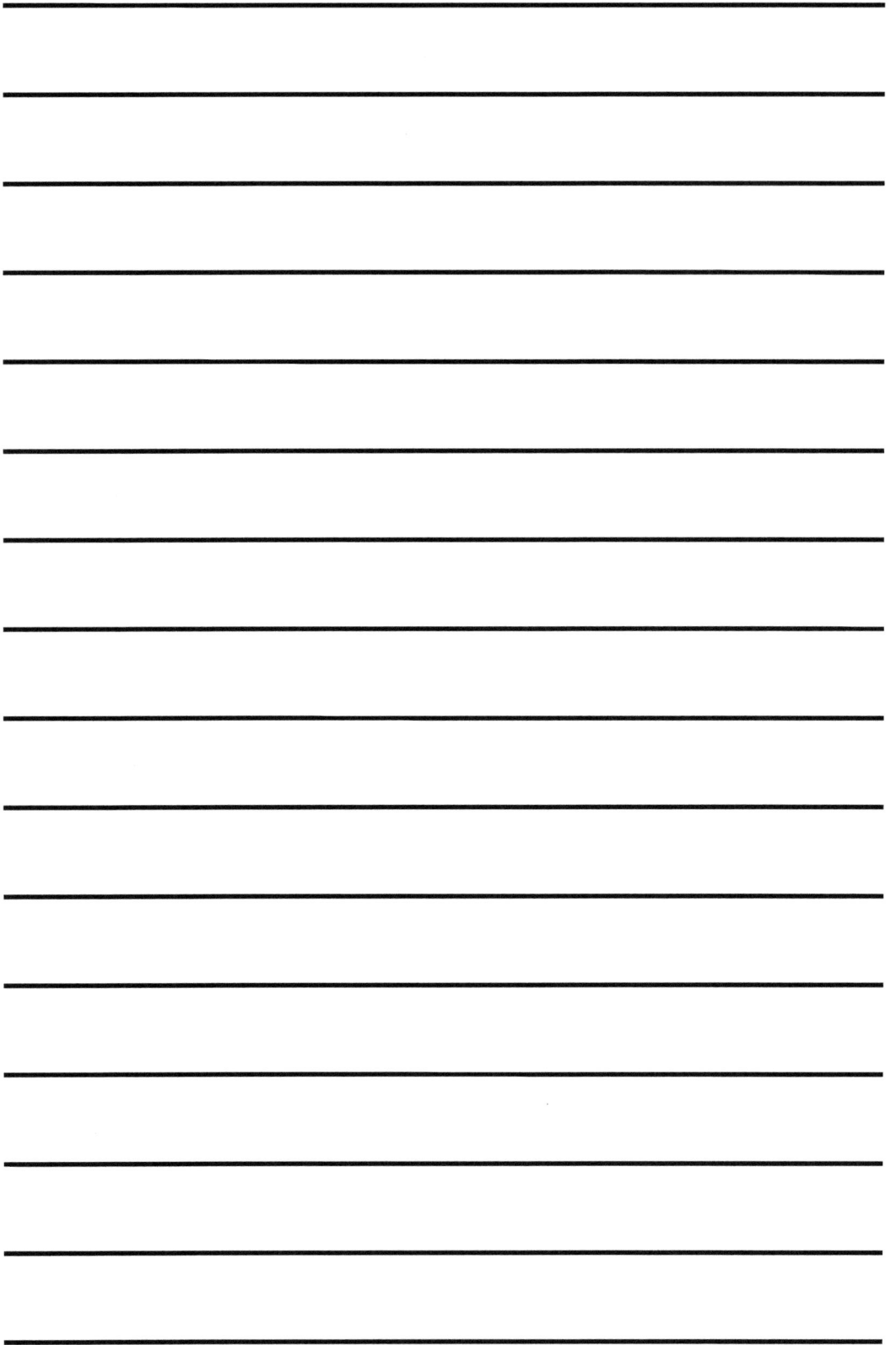

I LOVE THE SOUND OF CHURCH BELLS

THEY REACH EVERYONE THEY ARE NEAR,
NEVER SEGREGATING OR SEPARATING

THANK YOU FOR THE LIFE LONG SUPPLY OF

EMPTY CANVASES

YOU HAVE GIVEN US ALONG
THE SHORES OF THE WORLD

ANYTHING CAN BE DRAWN
– GOOD OR BAD –

ON THE FORGIVING SAND

AND IT WILL BE ERASED AND READY
FOR A NEW DRAWING EACH DAY

THANK YOU
FOR THE SCENT
THAT JUST A
SINGLE FLOWER
CAN GIVE

_____

_____

_____

_____

_____

_____

_____

_____

_____

_____

_____

_____

_____

_____

I AM SO GRATEFUL FOR SEA SHELLS WITH THEIR
ASTOUNDING DISPLAY OF RESILIENCE

EVEN WHEN CRUSHED INTO A FINE POWDER,
THEY HAVE THEIR IMPORTANCE AND PURPOSE

I AM ETERNALLY GRATEFUL FOR SONGWRITERS WHO GIVE US A PLACE TO EXIST WHEN NO ONE ELSE CAN UNDERSTAND US. THEY COMMISERATE WITH US WHEN WE FEEL ALONE. THEY GIFT US WITH SONG TO EASE OUR PAINS AND ENHANCE OUR JOYS

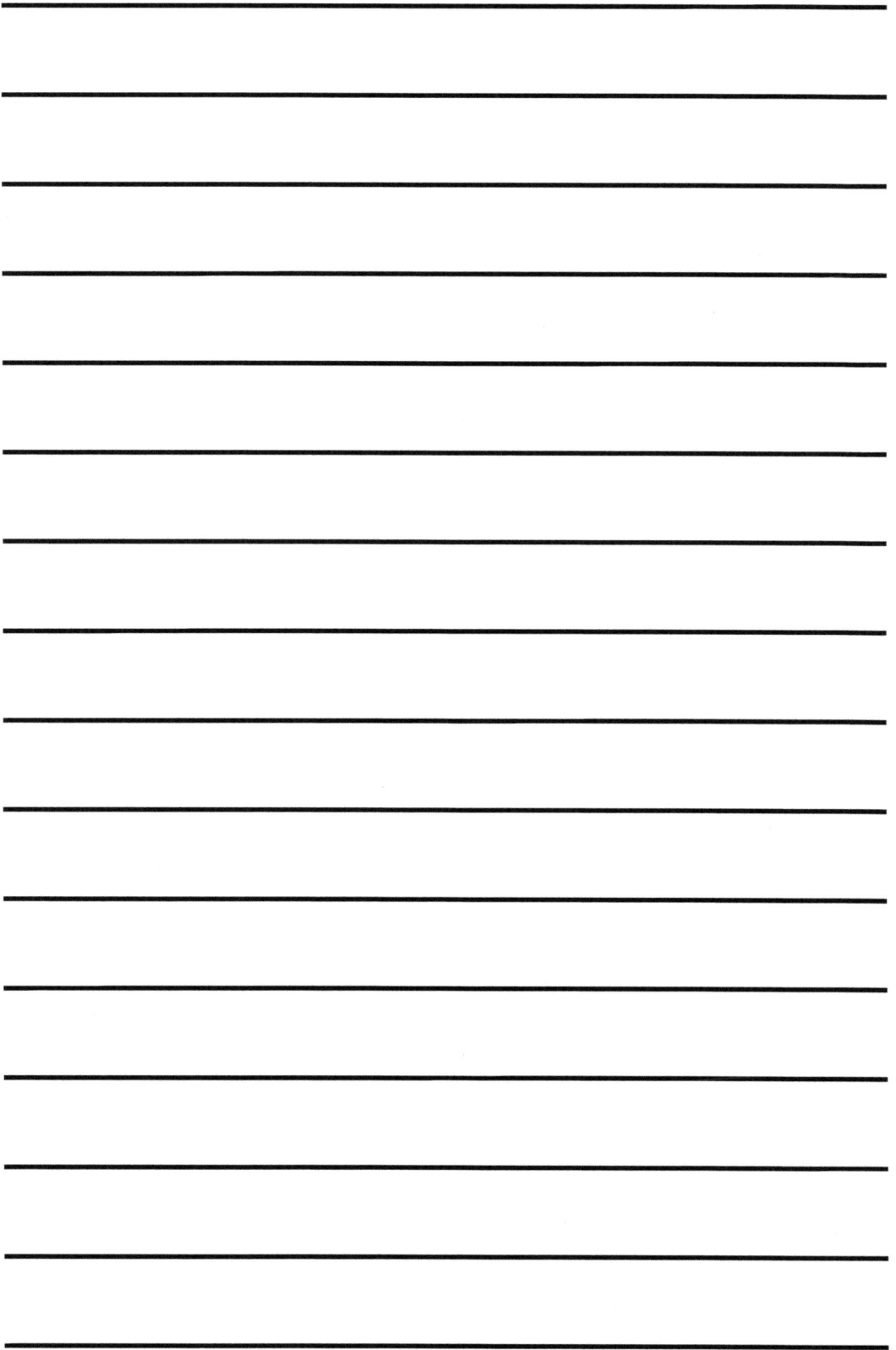

I AM SO VERY GRATEFUL FOR THE STILL
MOMENTS IN LIFE; THEY ARE WHAT ALLOW US TO
APPRECIATE JOYOUS MOMENTS

SOMETIMES WE CAN MISTAKE THEM FOR LIFE
BEING STAGNANT AND THINK OUR LIFE IS
GOING NOWHERE

IT IS IMPOSSIBLE TO SEE WHAT WONDERFUL
BEAUTIFUL THINGS LIE AHEAD

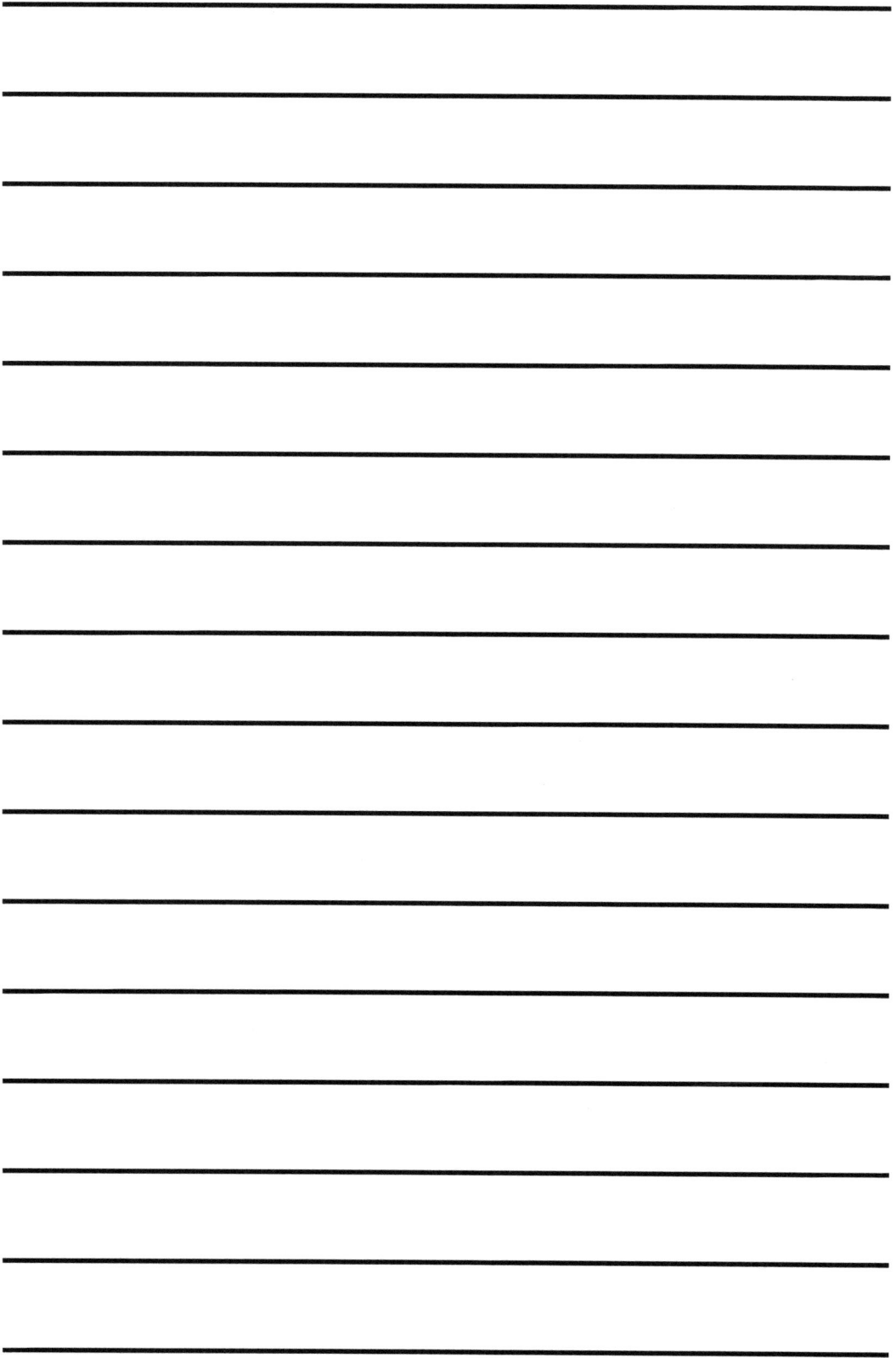

I LOVE HOW BIRDS GIFT US WITH THEIR SONG

THEY CHIRP LITTLE NOTES ANNOUNCING THE ARRIVAL OF SPRING AND SERENADE US ALL THROUGH THE SEASONS. I AM SO GRATEFUL FOR THESE LITTLE SOULS

I AM GRATEFUL FOR THE BLISS OF ROMANCE
AND THE BREATHTAKING FEELINGS WE GET TO ENJOY
WHEN WE EXPERIENCE LOVE

THERE IS SO MUCH LOVE IN THE TINIEST OF KISSES

EVEN THE SOFTEST LITTLE EMBRACE CAN GIVE US
SO
MUCH
DELIGHT

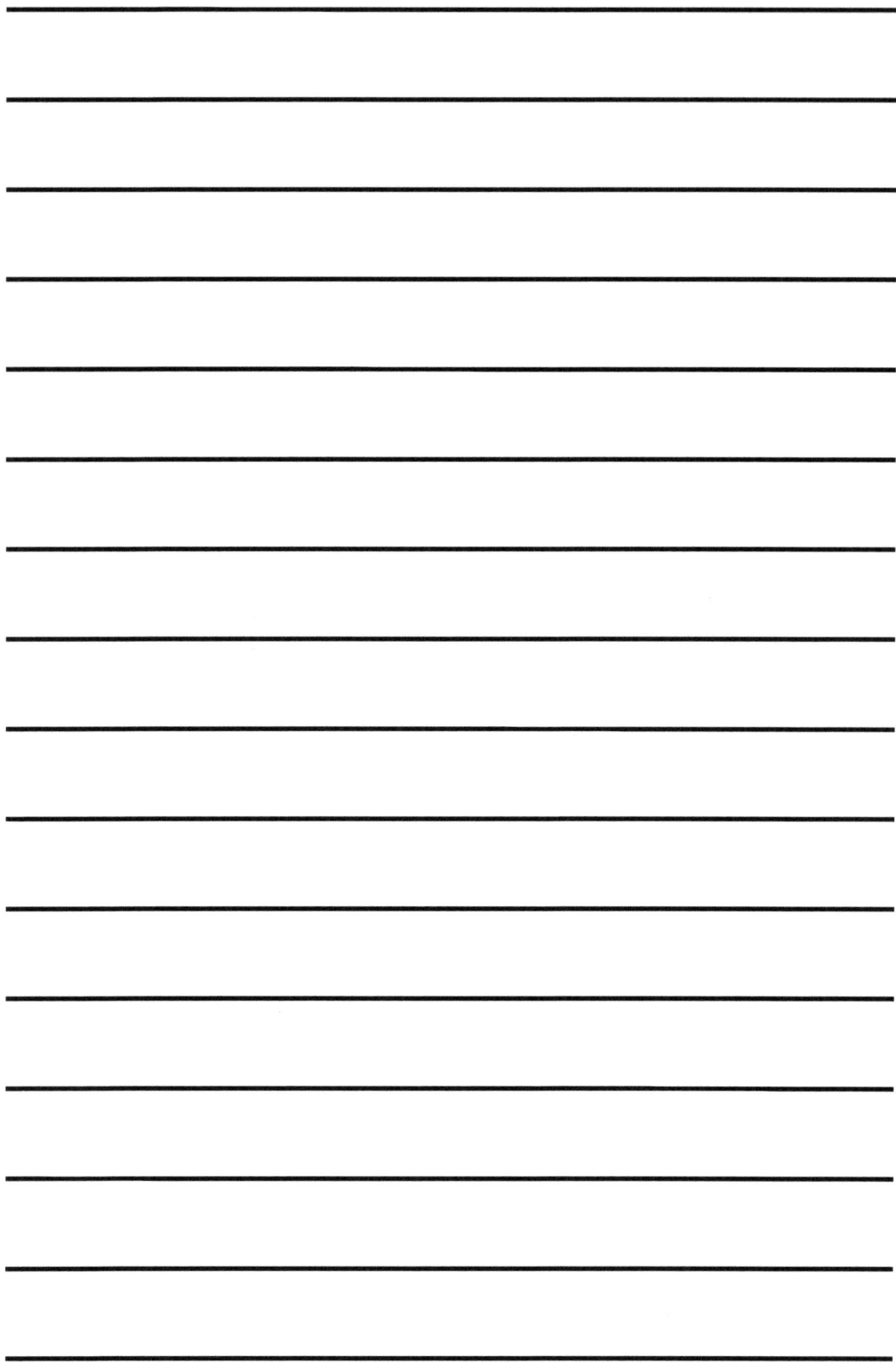

THANK YOU FOR THE BEAUTY THAT IS ALL AROUND US

IT IS EVERYWHERE, IN EVERYTHING,

WHEN WE TAKE THE TIME TO SEE IT

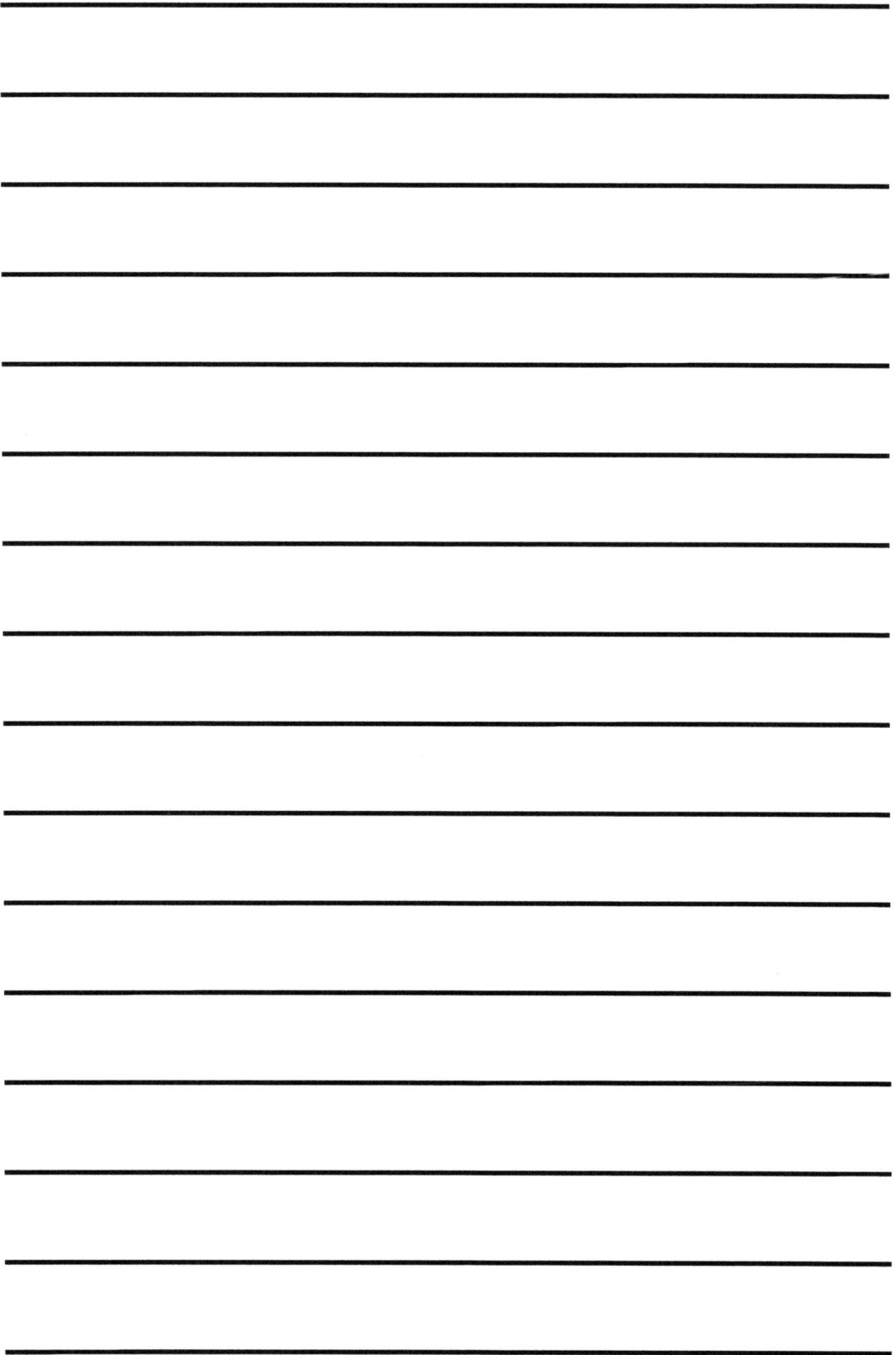

THANK YOU FOR ALL
THE GENTLE SIGNS
YOU LEAVE FOR US
EVERYWHERE

TO REMIND US THAT
WE ALL HAVE A
PLACE ON EARTH

WHATEVER OUR
SHAPE OR STATUS,
WITH OR WITHOUT
VOICE

WE ALL BELONG

EARTH BELONGS TO
ALL LIFE

THANK
YOU
FOR
OUR
HEART
BEAT

THE HEART
COULD HAVE
FUNCTIONED
SILENTLY

INSTEAD, IT
PROVIDES MUSIC

A DISTINCT
SONG FOR EACH
DISTINCT BEING

ALL A PART OF
ONE
VAST
RHYTHM

A CONTINUOUS
SYMPHONY

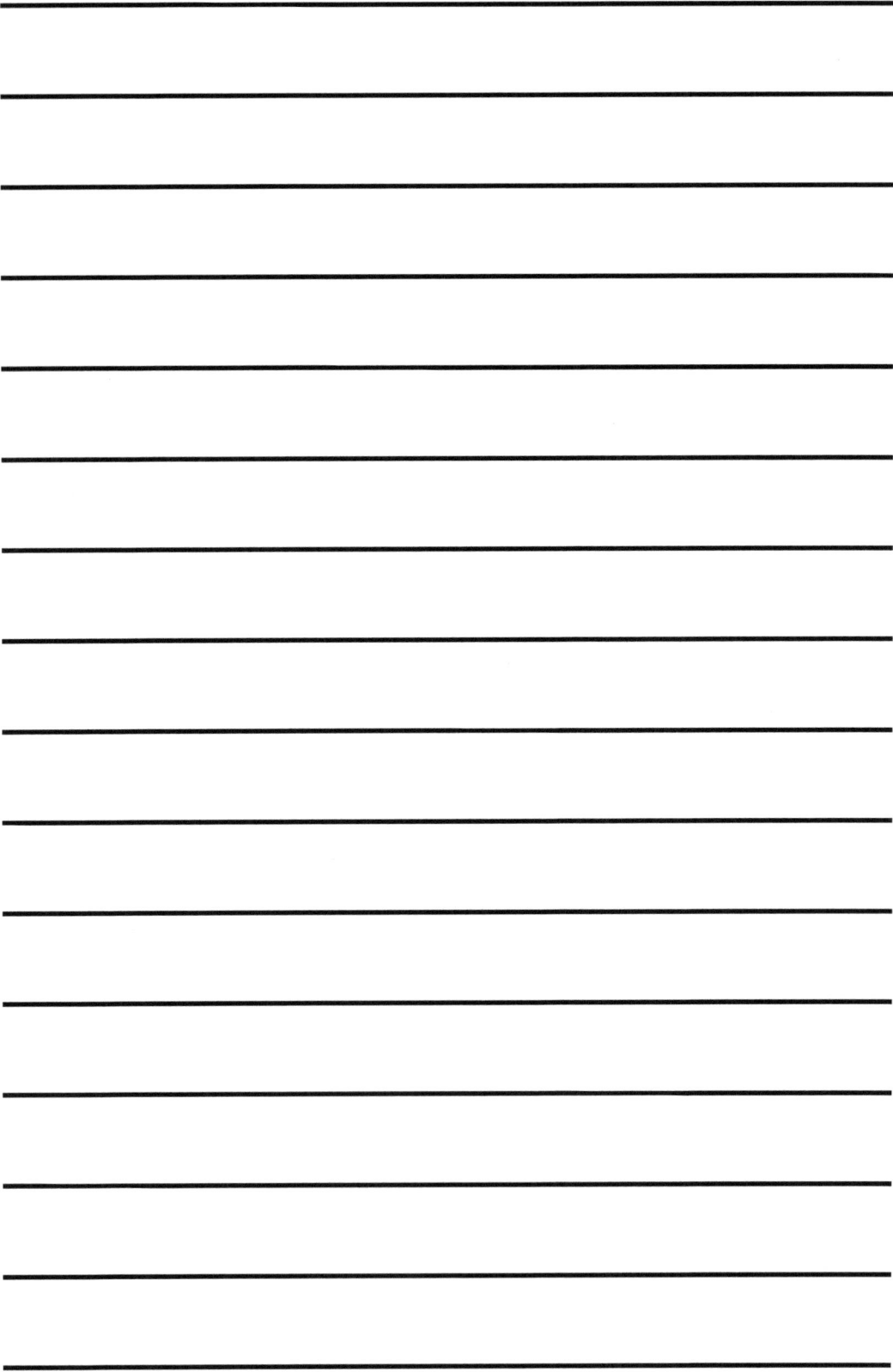

I AM SO GRATEFUL FOR
THE GENTLE BREEZES THAT
PROVIDE WARM CARESSES
AND ENVELOPE OUR BEING

THANK YOU FOR THE MIRACLES OF SUN
AND SNOW, WIND AND RAIN

THEY REMIND US THAT CHANGE,
EVEN IF IT IS SOMETIMES SCARY,
SOMETIMES COLD, IS A CRUCIAL AND
IMPORTANT PART OF OUR EXISTENCE

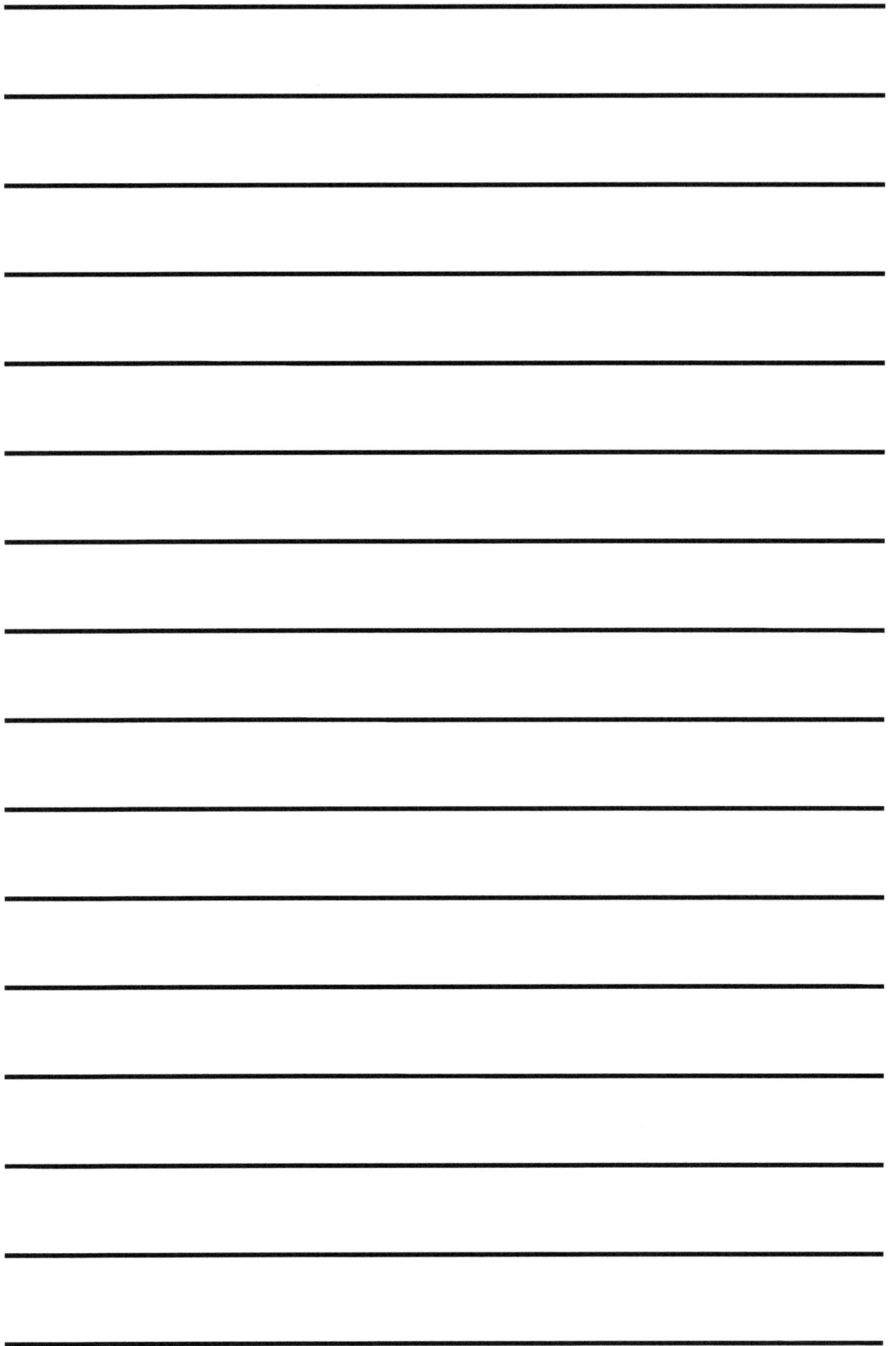

EVERY DAY I THANK THE KEEPERS OF THE
EARTH WHO LIVE IN THE VAST OCEANS
SURROUNDING US

THEY SILENTLY DO SO MUCH TO PROVIDE US
WITH A HABITABLE PLACE TO EXIST. MAY WE
ALL COME TO REALIZE AND APPRECIATE THEIR
VITAL IMPORTANCE AND PROTECT THEM

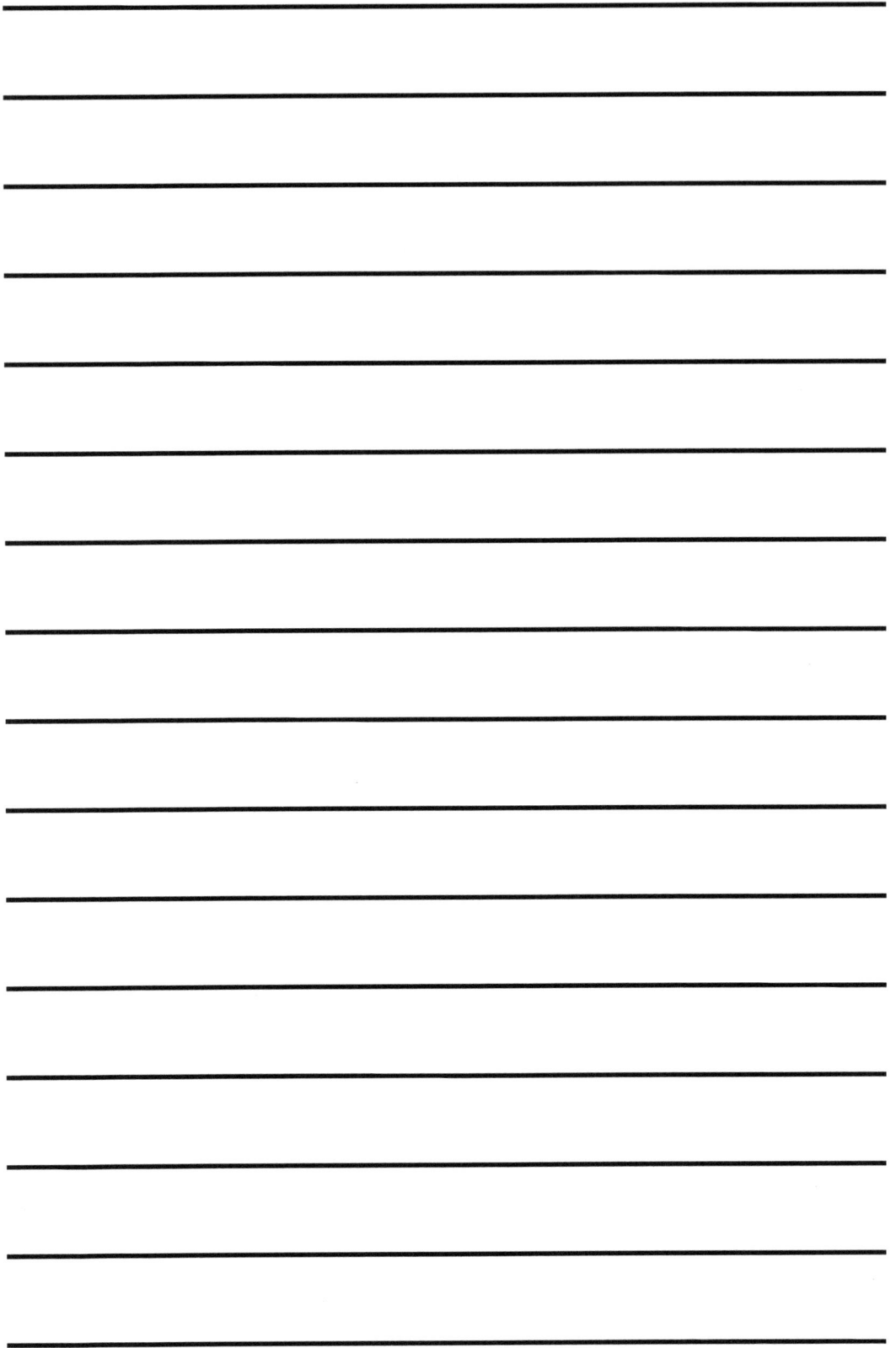

THANK YOU FOR LAZY DAYS WHEN I CAN JUST
SIT AND PONDER – GO INSIDE MYSELF,
REFLECT,
UNDERSTAND

THERE ARE BILLIONS OF THINGS HAPPENING EVERY
SECOND BUT I CAN BE STILL IN THIS ONE MOMENT

THIS
ONE
MOMENT
IS
MINE

ANY MOMENT I CHOOSE CAN BE MINE
THANK YOU FOR THESE MOMENTS

_____

_____

_____

_____

_____

_____

_____

_____

_____

_____

_____

_____

_____

_____

_____

_____

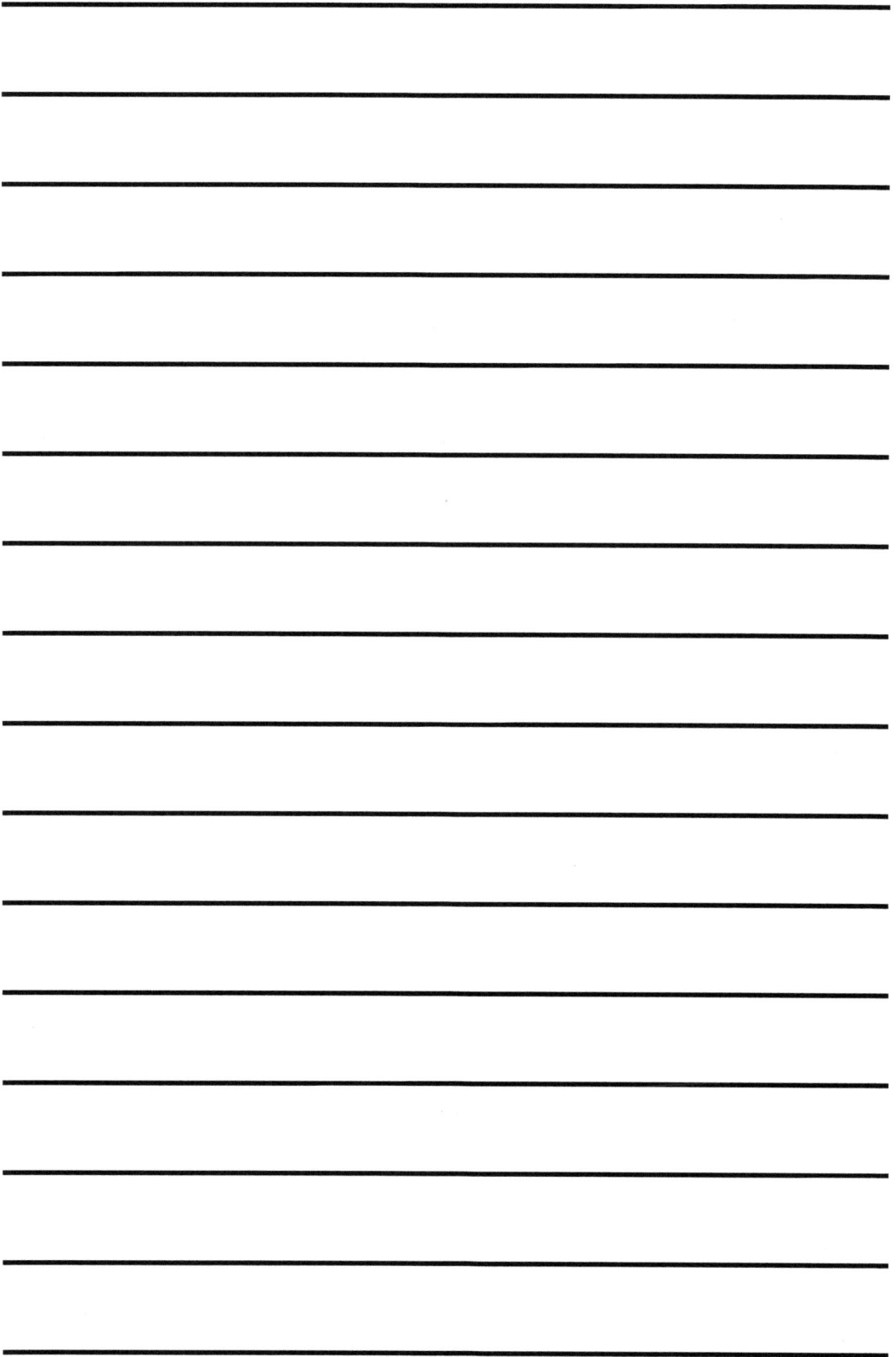

I AM INFINITELY GRATEFUL FOR

AUTHORS

WHO SHARE THEIR THOUGHTS AND
EXTRAORDINARY IMAGINATIONS WITH THE WORLD

THE MIRACLE OF BOOKS

WORDS

AND THEIR UNIQUE ABILITY TO MOVE
US AND ALLOW US TO IMAGINE

AND ASPIRE

THANK YOU FOR SILENCE,
ALWAYS THERE,
ALWAYS PROVIDING A PLACE OF SOLACE.

THANK *YOU* THE HOLDER OF THIS BOOK

I WISH YOU HAPPINESS IN EVERY MOMENT

Jaqui Karr

PRINTED IN THE UNITED STATES

ISBN: 978-0-9813198-5-8
FIRST REVISION

KARR, JAQUI:
        GRATITUDE IS THE ANSWER;
        THE SECRET TO HAPPINESS
        (DESKTOP VERSION)

LIBRARY AND ARCHIVES CANADA
BODY, MIND, AND SPIRIT

www.ingramcontent.com/pod-product-compliance
Lightning Source LLC
Chambersburg PA
CBHW061052090426
42740CB00003B/121